this journal belongs to

_____

Hi gorgeous! I'm Rachel, nice to meet you!

Hi pretty humans!

I am so glad you are here. Whether you struggle with some anxiety here and there, you're in therapy and want supplemental support outside of sessions or are well into your self-healing journal ready for fresh material on your path, I invite you to take this journal and make it a part of your next chapter.

It is my belief that this journal will enrich your life in so many ways, just like it has mine.

I have struggled with anxiety, depression, panic attacks, low self-worth, and eating disorder pathology for 16+ years.

Through therapy, research, and master's level psychology education, I have learned countless tools for managing, treating, and recovering from many of my symptoms. Still, there have been times where I felt traditional therapy was not enough, and I craved a consistent, daily practice to keep my symptoms at bay.

In 2018, my husband and I embarked on a year-long motorcycle adventure through Latin America. We sold all of our belongings and took to the open road. The journey was enthralling, eye-opening, and life changing.

Being on the road full-time revealed the gaping holes in my mental fitness: the daily uncertainty and lack of stability left me confronted with insecurities and anxieties I didn't know existed.

Traveling full-time humbled my recovery, and I knew if I was going to stay afloat amidst the constant change, I'd need a steady routine.

So I started journaling.

I didn't know where the practice would go or if it would help, but each morning, I took out my notebook and started writing affirmations, a practice I had learned in my Eating Disorder treatment program.

I started incorporating gratitude, a tool I had learned about in therapy.

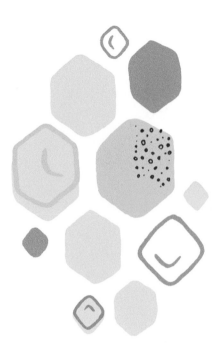

Slowly, other prompts found their way into my daily ritual. I drew on the concepts of Dialectical Behavior Therapy, Zen Mindfulness, Spiritual Psychology, and holistic practices.

With a simple journaling practice, I was coping ahead for stressful situations, manifesting dreams and goals, writing power mantras, and harnessing a new type of self-love I hadn't previously experienced.

Within a few months, the constant uncertainty of my life no longer sent me into a panic attack.

The desire to have space and "me" time felt like a gift I was giving myself, not a burden on my relationships.

I experienced more joy, more abundance, and a sense of soulful connection to myself I had never found— not even through a decade of therapy.

This journal is the compilation of a year's worth of journaling: it is the same rubric I used daily, and encompasses the tools, practices, and exercises I have learned over the course of a decade, boiled down into a brief, daily practice.

Whether you stumbled upon this journal in your quest for self-discovery, or felt called to enrich your existing healing journey with a robust daily practice, **this journal is for you.**

Welcome to the next chapter in your life.

XO,

Rachel Havekost

what you'll find in this journal

Your guide to a fucking rad, self-loving, soulfully manifested, and grateful-as-hell-life.

what is the self-healer's journal?

The Self-Healer's Journal is not your typical "Dear Diary" moment. While free-writing is a beautiful practice, guided journaling (the type of journaling you will experience here) is a more intentional, thought-provoking experience.

The Self-Healer's Journal will invite you to **reflect, create, or re-frame your thinking** based on prompts, questions, or specific activities.

You will be presented with specific categories like **mindfulness, gratitude, affirmations, and more**. Each day, you will have different prompts or instructions within each category.

When you practice guided journaling, you are **allowing yourself to flow into new ways of thinking, feeling, and seeing yourself** in the world.

You will **open yourself up to possibilities** you never knew existed, and **tap into inner knowings** about yourself that have been there all along.

how do I do it?

Just begin. Each daily journal only takes about 12 minutes. That's about as long as it takes me to drink a cup of coffee, so I am confident you can fit this into your morning (or daily) routine.

No matter what, **give yourself grace and permission** to be imperfect. I intentionally did not have the days in this journal align with specific dates, because if you miss a day, I don't want you to see an empty page in your journal and feel shame for missing a day. It's ok. **You're human**. You are doing the best you can, and I love you for it!

It is up to you when you start, and to **trust your intuition** to tell you how often to practice. There is no law or regulation on how often you are meant to journal: **this is your practice**, nobody else's.

Each day will consist of **four prompts**. The prompts are recycled daily, and I have mixed and matched the categories for you. **No two days will be the same**, and there will be instances where you get to pick what you journal about. You always have the **option to change the prompt** if it's not vibing with you that day!

Every day starts with mindfulness, which is a beautiful way to get grounded and relieve yourself of distractions before doing the rest of the journaling prompts (you can find more instructions and guidance on mindfulness in the pages to come).

The prompts will have **clear instructions** for how to respond in the journal and the spaces provided. Many of the prompts are meant to elicit brief, list-like responses, which make it **simple, fast, and easy**.

My practice is daily (with lots of permission for days off if I'm just not up for it). **I like to journal first thing in the morning** with my cup of coffee, as it puts my mind in a positive, calm place for the rest of the day.

Whenever you choose to practice, here are my tips for how to make the most of this journal:

tip 01

Read the category descriptions so you can fully understand the purpose, utility, and language of the prompts you will encounter. You can find a full description of each category on page 10.

tip 02

Create a "Ritual Space." I highly recommend creating a ritual space—a place in your home, a time of day, and using the five senses to create a full, experiential "space" that becomes your journaling time and spot. My ritual space includes a cozy nook wherever I am (I travel full time so it's not always the same), takes place first thing in the morning, and is accompanied with soft music, the warmth and smell of my coffee, and a pretty candle if I have access to one.

tip 03

Turn off your phone or other notifications, and ask anyone you live with not to bother you while you write in your journal. The more uninterrupted this experience, the deeper flow you will come in contact with, and the richer the experience will be.

tip 04

You will be asked to write your mood at the beginning and the end of each entry. There is a feelings wheel on page 8, this will help you start to identify your feelings and label them as you embark on this journey.

tip 05

If you struggle with any of the prompts, I invite you to practice self-compassion. Be kind to yourself. It's ok if some of these don't come naturally—that's why it's a practice! It's something to return to, try again, and to learn and grow from. This is not a test, competition, or chore—it is simply a practice.

BONUS TIP: Try it with a partner or friend & share out loud.

feelings wheel

Use this feelings wheel to identify your emotions.

the outermost feelings are heightened, magnified, or specific versions of their core emotion

start by asking yourself:

"what am I feeling in this moment?"

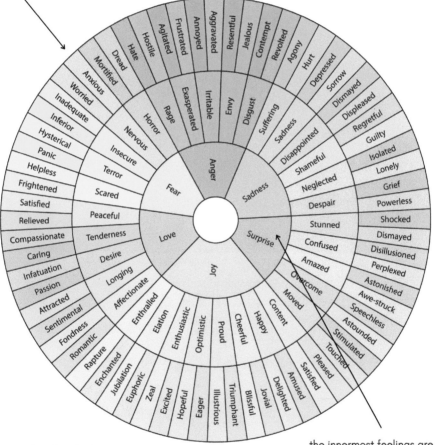

once you've identified your feelings, you can trace each emotion back to a "core" emotion

the innermost feelings are "core emotions"

this feelings wheel was created by the junto institute

example of a daily journal

In the next few pages, I'll provide detailed descriptions and support for each prompt and category you might see in this journal.

today's date: APRIL 15

Starting mood: ANXIOUS, OVERWHELMED, DISCOURAGED

Ending mood: CALM, ENERGIZED, POWERFUL

Mindfulness: Object Observation. Set a timer for one minute. Choose an object in your line of sight. Using "beginner's mind," try to remain non-judgmental, meaning not adding any qualitative words to the observations you make. When the timer goes off, jot down what the experience was like for you.

I NOTICED IT WAS HARD FOR ME TO STAY FOCUSED, MY THOUGHTS KEPT DRIFTING OFF. I TRIED JUST NOTICING THEM, ESPECIALLY WHEN I FOUND MYSELF THINKING, "I'M NOT DOING THIS RIGHT." I TRIED TO JUST NOTICE THOSE THOUGHTS AND LET THEM FLOAT ON, AND THEN COME BACK TO OBSERVING THE OBJECT.

Gratitude: This Past Month. List six things you are grateful for from this past month.

I'M GRATEFUL TO MY BROTHER IN-LAW FOR ALLOWING ME TO STAY IN HIS HOME WHILE I TRANSITION HOUSING.

I'M SO GRATEFUL IT HAS BEEN SUNNY AND WARM, WHICH HAS ALLOWED ME TO GO OUTSIDE AND APPRECIATE NATURE WHERE I LIVE.

I'M GRATEFUL I HAVE BEEN ABLE TO FIND FREELANCE WORK AND PAY MY BILLS!

I'M GRATEFUL TO MY PAST CLIENTS FOR REFERRING ME TO MORE AMAZING, IDEAL CLIENTS!

I'M GRATEFUL THAT MY ANKLE HAS HEALED SO WELL AND I'VE BEEN ABLE TO RUN AGAIN!

Affirmations: Talents and Skills. Make six affirmations about your talents and skills.

I AM REALLY TALENTED AT WRITING.

I'M A SKILLED ARTIST AND I MAKE BEAUTIFUL SKETCHES!

I'M A NATURAL WHEN IT COMES TO LEARNING AND PLAYING BOARD GAMES.

I'M REALLY GOOD AT UNDERSTANDING PEOPLE AND THEIR EMOTIONS.

I'M SKILLED IN LISTENING AND EMPATHIZING WITH OTHERS!

Power Mantras for Wisdom: Write two power mantras about your inner wisdom.

I HAVE DEEP, INNER KNOWING ABOUT WHAT I DESERVE.

I CAN TAP INTO MY WISDOM AT ANY TIME.

journaling categories

On the next several pages you'll find descriptions for each journaling category and instructions for using the prompts in your journaling templates.

01 mindfulness

Mindfulness is the art of painting without a plan. Singing without lyrics. Observing without changing. Mindfulness opens our minds to the possibility that there is no right or wrong way to do, be, think, or feel: everything just "is."

Mindfulness can be a daunting practice for many people—I know it was for me. When I first learned what mindfulness was, my type-A, sun-in-Capricorn, moon-in-Virgo brain was like "LOL, cute, you want me to WHAT?"

The idea of slowing down, focusing on one thing in the moment, and simply noticing (rather than evaluating) what I was doing seemed nonsensical.

I also thought there was only one way to practice mindfulness. I pictured cross-legged hippies with their hands on their laps, ohm-ing and chanting for hours on end. I didn't know the difference between mindfulness and meditation, nor did I realize there were even different branches of mindfulness.

While in therapy, I learned that practicing mindfulness was not, in fact, the same as meditation, nor did it have to be some big to-do. We would start every therapy session with some form of mindfulness, and I learned the practice could be simple and approachable.

Mindfulness, when used daily, can drastically improve your ability to free yourself from judgment, let go of attachments, and allow life to just "be."

- Many of the exercises in this journal come from Zen Mindfulness, which is the act of non-judgmental awareness. By connecting to your senses, noticing what's in your surroundings, and accepting your thoughts and feelings non-judgmentally, you learn to witness the world as an unbiased observer.

While practicing Mindfulness, I invite you to keep the following in mind:

- There is no right or wrong way to practice mindfulness. Practice freeing yourself from "how" the task is done, or whether it is correct. However you do it is the right way. This is the art of non-attachment: we release our expectations of how something is "intended" to turn out. By allowing space for any and all outcomes, we learn to reduce anxiety, anticipation, or disappointment in our lives. We become more flexible and able to adapt to uncertainty and change.

- If you notice your thoughts trailing away from the exercise, or if you become distracted, simply notice it, and return your mind back to the task at hand.

- In mindfulness, "judgments" are used to describe all adjectives or descriptions of an experience or object—not just negative evaluations. The goal in mindfulness is to let go of all judgments, both positive and negative. In doing so, we allow ourselves to see things just as they are, without any evaluation. Notice any "judgments" that arise as you practice mindfulness, observing them and slowly letting them float away.

Rachel's tip: Try using "beginner's mind," meaning you treat the activity as if you were a newborn baby, engaging with the task for the very first time.

gratitude

Gratitude begets gratitude. Practicing gratitude is a magical way to bring joy and peace into your life. Intentionally practicing gratitude, no matter how big or small, creates more moments of spontaneous gratitude.

Gratitude is the practice of reflecting on or naming what you are thankful for. This can be events in your life, objects or material items, people and relationships, experiences, nature, gifts, talents...the list goes on.

Once you start practicing gratitude, you will notice a shift in your mindset: experiences that are normally dull or boring become exciting and invigorating. You'll begin to train your mind to see the joy, spark, and wonder in every little aspect of your life.

Nothing is too small to be grateful for. Gratitude is not always about the big stuff—gratitude for the little things is what creates more and sustaining joy all day for all things.

Example gratitude statement: *"I am SO grateful that I have a big, fat, cuddly dog to keep me company at night."*

While practicing Gratitude. I invite you to keep the following in mind:

- When writing your gratitude statements, I encourage you to ALWAYS begin with "I am grateful for" or "I am grateful to," etc, rather than just listing what you are grateful for.

- Be specific. Instead of, "I am grateful that I have a job," try, "I am grateful that I have a steady, stable job that I am good at." Why? Because gratitude breeds more of what you are grateful for. If you specify what it is about your job you are grateful for, that is what you will find more of in your life.

- Don't take this or yourself too seriously. Find humor. Be silly. You can be grateful for random crap and you can make gratitude statements about that one nose hair that keeps growing back. This is about generating self-love, excitement, and JOY in your life. It is about getting more grounded in YOUR skin—it is NOT about making you someone or something you're not. So make this yours.

03 affirmations

Affirmations are a self-loather's nightmare. They are also a self-loather's greatest medicine. Affirmations are statements about oneself that are true or that one hopes to be true.

Affirmations can be a challenge for those who struggle with low self-esteem. They are one of the hardest exercises in a journaling practice because they work the hardest.

With regular practice, affirmations can become the most pivotal tool in your transformation towards self-love, acceptance, and buttloads of confidence.

Affirmations can be written many different ways, so again remember there is no "right" way to do this. You can think of affirmations as compliments, confidence-boosting statements, or beliefs.

Affirmations are about yourself: they are statements that typically begin with "I" or "I am," and they are meant to uplift, inspire, and encourage you.

Example affirmation statement: *"I have the body of a goddess, and I treat it as such!"*

While doing Affirmations, I invite you to keep the following in mind:

- Affirm qualities about yourself, rather than possessions or accolades. (i.e. "I have a really cool bicycle" is not an affirmation that will help you build self-worth/esteem. It might make your bike feel really good, which is nice, but this is for you, not your bike.)

- Make affirmations that you are working towards. For example, if you wish you were more confident, make an affirmation like, "I am working every day on building my confidence."

- Make affirmations that you might not fully believe now, but want to. Even if you don't believe it now, you can still make the affirmation, "I am a confident person," and eventually, you'll believe it.

- If you get stuck, think about what a loved one might say about you. Sometimes I like to think about what my therapist would say about me if I was having a hard time coming up with an answer to a prompt.

Rachel's tip: *Get creative. Rather than just saying "I am happy," try "I am full of joy, abundance, and energy!"*

04 power mantras

Power Mantras are statements that give you chills. Statements about yourself or your life that are so powerful, you feel like a superhero saying them. They are brave, bold, and short enough to remember throughout the day. The more you practice them, the more they stir up feelings of invincibility in you.

Power mantras are meant to be short and sweet. The shorter and more memorable they are, the more powerful they become. If you can't remember the mantra after reading it once, it's probably too long.

Power mantras are meant to be called on throughout the day: They serve as pre-made, energizing shots that you can toss back at any point in your day.

Example power mantra: *"I am a force of positive and loving energy!"*

While doing Power Mantras, I invite you to keep the following in mind:

- If you get stuck, try starting with, "I have the power to..."

- These can be vague or specific—you could have a mantra like, "I will create greatness in my life," or "My resilience is on fire."

- Imagine you are someone who you look up to while writing the mantra: call in their language and tone of voice when thinking of your wording.

Rachel's tip: Stand in a superhero position while you think of your power mantra.

05 manifestation statements

Manifestation is the concept of putting an idea or dream into the universe by saying it aloud, and in doing so creating energy and causation for it to occur. Build a practice of creating your own manifestation statements so you can call in exactly what you want in life.

Manifestation statements are phrases that have to do with specific things you want to bring into in your life: abundance, a community of like-minded people, a trip, a program you're creating... You'll make simple statements that are specific and related to some goal or ultimate desire.

Many of us have big dreams, but we never say them aloud. When you put your dreams into words, onto paper, and tell someone about them, the universe listens. If I keep saying "I always get picked last in kickball," the universe hears me, and says, "yes, yes you do." But if I start saying, "I always get picked first in kickball," the universe hears me and says, "oh, shit. We didn't know that, sorry, we'll start to make some changes so that can happen."

The trick with manifestation is repetition, patience, and faith. Once you start to observe small ways you manifest things in your life, you will start to notice how much you truly manifest on a day to day basis.

Example Manifestation mantra: *"By the end of this year, I will have written and published a book that connects millions of women through shared experiences."*

While doing Manifestation Statements, I invite you to keep the following in mind:

- Think of something you really, really, really want, even if you haven't figured out how you're going to get it.

- Get specific. Set a date, a year, a time frame. "In the next 12 months, I will have completed my Yoga Certification."

- It's OK if the manifestation doesn't become 100% true. The idea is to put the energy of what you want OUT THERE, so that some part of what you hope to achieve begins to churn.

- Don't get caught up on what's logical or realistic. Dream, dare, imagine.

Rachel's tip: *If you get stuck, try drawing a picture of your future. What did you draw? Who is there? Use insights from this drawing to write a manifestation statement.*

06 expectations & mini-mantras

No one can predict the future, and yet we make expectations daily of what we believe will or will not happen. By naming our expectations, we can set ourselves up to be gentle if life has another plan. This teaches us to be flexible, adaptable, and self-compassionate in the face of life's inevitable unknowns.

While traveling for over a year, I learned quickly that I had to constantly renegotiate my expectations of what I thought I was doing each day, as things often didn't go according to plan.

To fend off disappointment or anxiety, I now create a daily list of my "expectations"—things I think are going to happen that day or things I want to happen. This can range from activities to stressors—sometimes I'll write that I expect to get anxious, which I may want to have a mantra set up for.

After making that list, I write a short "mini-mantra"— a small statement or mini-mantra that I can tell myself later in the day if/when my expectation does or does not happen.

Example Expectation & Mini-Mantra::
expectation: I'll write a blog post.
mini-mantra: Writing is fun for you—if it feels forced, you don't have to do it.

While doing Expectations & Mini-Mantras, I invite you to keep the following in mind:

- Don't overthink it. If you aren't aware of what your daily expectations are right away, just ask yourself, "what do I hope happens today?" or "what do I expect to obviously happen today?"

- Keep your mini-mantras short and simple.

- If you can't think of a mini-mantra, try just using "if this doesn't go the way I hoped, that will be ok."

Rachel's tip: *Mark which of the expectations are really important to you. Then use the re-frame section as an option to say something like, "this is really important to me, so I'll prioritize it today." You can then easily shift into re-framing what is less important by saying, "if I don't get to this today, that's ok. It wasn't a priority anyway."*

07 letters to yourself

Writing a letter to yourself is a practice in self-compassion. Some days, it can feel impossible to be kind to ourselves. These are the days we need self-compassion the most.

Every so often, your only journaling task of the day will be to write a letter to yourself. The invitation will be to write to yourself in a kind, compassionate, and loving way.

By writing yourself a letter, you get the opportunity to look at yourself from an outside perspective. You'll find new ways to speak to yourself that may be difficult to unlock when writing daily affirmations.

Example letter I wrote to myself:

Dear Rachel, I know this is a crazy time. You just moved across the globe in the middle of a pandemic, you're living with your husband for the first time in five months, you're in a new place that isn't yours, you have a ton of writing and shit feels crazy. I know you want to do it all, and I admire you for that. But it's ok to take a break. It's ok to slow down. Life will unfold as it's meant to unfold. The things you feel anxious about are all fabrications anyway—it's all made up. This planet is just a floating star, a piece of dust, and you are too—a star, a small moving part of something greater. You are a part of something greater. You are a part of something big—so big you can't see it. So if you take one day "off," one day to rest, reflect, be still or do "nothing," the universe won't shatter. Because you are not the only part—we are all tiny little fragments, working in tandem and flow to move the universe on her path. Or maybe it's she that moves us, and we are silly to think we had any power all along. And in fact, this ache you have to stop or slow down is the universe telling you, "Be peace. Be still. You are the restful star, now, and I will call when it is time again for you to move with a brisk agenda."

While writing a letter to yourself, I invite you to keep the following in mind:

- What tone would you use if you were writing a letter to a younger version of yourself?

- What language would you use if you were trying to be kind?

- How can you be understanding and compassionate, but still offer wisdom and knowing?

Rachel's tip: Let your pen flow. No one else is reading this but you, and it is for nobody else but you. It's like little love notes from self to self.

90 days
of journaling

before you begin this transformation...

take a moment
to reflect

Setting intentions is a wonderful way to begin a new practice with clarity, alignment, and commitment. Before beginning on this adventure, take a moment to reflect on why you are here.

What are your intentions for this journal? Why is this practice important to you, and what do you hope to gain?

checklist

It's time to get started! Before beginning, make sure you've completed each item below so you can get the most out of this journal.

- [ ] I've read through each category description

- [ ] I've written down my intentions on page 27 and how I'm feeling at the start of this journey

- [ ] I've seen an example journal filled out on page 9 so I have a framework for the templates

- [ ] I know where the feelings wheel is on page 8 and how to use it as a reference when I do my mood check

- [ ] I believe I am a kickass human for investing in myself and this journal

- [ ] I love myself no matter how this goes, and will always love myself no matter what

day 01

*"You yourself, as much as anybody in the entire universe,
deserve your love and affection."*
-Buddha

starting mood: _____

today's date: _____   ending mood: _____

Mindfulness: *Energy Ball.* Sit in a comfortable position with your legs and arms uncrossed, eyes closed. Starting with your toes, imagine a warm ball of energy moving up your body. Once the energy ball reaches the top of your head, return it to your third eye center (the space between your eyebrows). Imagine the ball of energy and visualize what color it is. Jot down what the experience was like in the space below.

Gratitude: *Abilities.* List six abilities you have that you are grateful for and why.

Affirmations: *Worth.* Make six affirmations about your worth.

Power Mantras for Letting Go: Write two power mantras that have to do with surrender, letting go, and radical acceptance.

day 02

*"Live as if you were living a second time, and as though
you had acted wrongly the first time."*
-Viktor Frankl

starting mood: _____

today's date: _____   ending mood: _____

Mindfulness: *Object Sensory Observation.* Set a timer for one minute. Pick up an object near you and close your eyes. Using "beginner's mind," imagine you are feeling this object for the first time. After the minute is up, jot down what the experience was like for you in the space below.

Gratitude: *Abilities.* List six abilities you have that you are grateful for and why.

Affirmations: *Freebie.* Make your own category or prompts for what you will write affirmations about, and write four affirmations based on that category below.

Month Ahead Manifestations: Think of something specific you hope to achieve. Maybe it's a dream you've had for a long time. Maybe it's a new goal you're working towards. Make statements like, "I will," or "I am going to," rather than "I hope to," or "I want to." Be specific with timing and words. Write it down in the space below. Say it out loud three times to really send it out into the universe.

day 03

"Accept yourself; then others will."

starting mood: _____

today's date: _____

ending mood: _____

Mindfulness: *Connect the Dots. Starting from the left of the box below, connect the dots from left to right without lifting your pen from the page. You can draw up, down, diagonally, backward, and forward. Try to focus on each dot as you connect them. If your thoughts wander or if you notice yourself starting to make judgments, simply notice those thoughts and return to connecting the dots.*

· ·
· ·
· ·
· ·

Gratitude: *Opportunities.* List four opportunities you have had or are going to have that you are grateful for.

Affirmations: *Appearance.* Make six affirmations about your appearance.

Power Mantras for Your Worth: Write two power mantras about your worthiness as a human being.

day 04

"What is coming is better than what is gone."
-Arabic Proverb

today's date: _____

starting mood: _____
ending mood: _____

Mindfulness: *Sound Observation.* Set a timer for one minute. Close your eyes. Listen to all the sounds around you. Try to remain non-judgmental, meaning not adding any qualitative words to the sounds you hear. When the timer goes off, jot down what the experience was like for you.

Gratitude: *Yesterday.* List four things you are grateful for from yesterday.

Affirmations: *Talents and Skills.* Make six affirmations about your talents and skills.

Manifestation Statement: Make one, powerful statement about what you hope to manifest for your self-worth. Write it three times, each time making the words bigger on the page.

day 05

"Make happiness a priority and be gentle with yourself in the process."
-Bronnie Ware

starting mood: _____

today's date: _____   ending mood: _____

Mindfulness: *Object Naming.* Set a timer for one minute. Look all around you, and in your mind, list everything you see. Try to remain non-judgmental, meaning not adding any qualitative words to the objects you see. After the minute is up, jot down what the experience was like for you in the space below.

Gratitude: *Occupation.* Think of four things you are grateful for about your job, school, retirement, or unemployment.

Affirmations: Complete the following affirmations:

I am:

I have a beautiful:

I excel at:

I love my:

I am really good at:

I am skilled at:

Expectations   **Mini-Mantras**

day 06

"Expectations are resentments waiting to happen."
-Brene Brown

starting mood: _____

today's date: _____   ending mood: _____

Mindfulness: *Free Doodle.* Set a timer for one minute. Doodle in the space provided. If your thoughts wander or if you notice yourself starting to make judgments about your doodling, simply notice those thoughts and return your attention to your drawing.

Gratitude: *Relationships.* List six people you are grateful for, and why.

Affirmations: *Personality.* Make six affirmations about your personality.

Power Mantras for Letting Go: Write two power mantras that have to do with surrender, letting go, and radical acceptance.

day 07

"The greater your storm the brighter your rainbow."

Mindfulness: *Connect the Dots. Starting from the left of the box below, connect the dots from left to right without lifting your pen from the page. You can draw up, down, diagonally, backward, and forward. Try to focus on each dot as you connect them. If your thoughts wander or if you notice yourself starting to make judgments, simply notice those thoughts and return to connecting the dots.*

· ·
· ·
· ·
· ·

Gratitude: *Variety Pack.* List what you are grateful for in the following six categories.

Affirmations: *Talents and Skills.* Make six affirmations about your talents and skills.

Exponential Manifestation Statements: Think of something you'd like to accomplish in the next year. Get specific. Use the SAME GOAL for all three statements: they are each more powerful than the previous.
In the next year, I want to...

In the next year I will...

By the end of this year, I will...

day 08

"To fall in love with yourself is the first secret to happiness."
-Robert Morely

starting mood: _____

today's date: _____   ending mood: _____

Mindfulness: *Sound Observation. Set a timer for one minute. Close your eyes. Listen to all the sounds around you. Try to remain non-judgmental, meaning not adding any qualitative words to the sounds you hear. When the timer goes off, jot down what the experience was like for you.*

Gratitude: *Yesterday.* List four things you are grateful for from yesterday.

Affirmations: *Appearance.* Make six affirmations about your appearance.

Power Mantras for Letting Go: Write two power mantras that have to do with surrender, letting go, and radical acceptance.

day 09

"Don't let your mind bully your body."
-June Tomaso Wood

today's date: _____

Mindfulness: *Object Observation.* Set a timer for one minute. Choose an object in your line of sight. Using "beginner's mind," try to remain non-judgmental, meaning not adding any qualitative words to the observations you make. When the timer goes off, jot down what the experience was like for you.

Gratitude: *This Past Year.* List six things you are grateful for from this past year.

Affirmations: *Freebie.* Make your own category or prompts for what you will write affirmations about and write four affirmations based on that category below.

Month Ahead Manifestations: Think of something specific you hope to achieve. Maybe it's a dream you've had for a long time. Maybe it's a new goal you're working towards. Make statements like, "I will," or "I am going to," rather than "I hope to," or "I want to." Be specific with timing and words. Write it down in the space below. Say it out loud three times to really send it out into the universe.

day 10

"Worrying won't stop bad stuff from happening. It just keeps you from enjoying the good."

Mindfulness: *Object Sensory Observation.* Set a timer for one minute. Pick up an object near you and close your eyes. Using "beginner's mind," imagine you are feeling this object for the first time. After the minute is up, jot down what the experience was like for you in the space below.

Gratitude: *Occupation.* Think of four things you are grateful for about your job, school, retirement, or unemployment.

Affirmations: *Talents and Skills.* Make six affirmations about your talents and skills.

Expectations   **Mini-Mantras**

day 11

"Don't let perfect be the enemy of good."
-Sheri Salata

starting mood: _____

today's date: _____   ending mood: _____

Letter to Yourself: What Do I Need to Hear? Ask yourself, "what do I need right now?" Write the answer at the top of the page, then write yourself a letter responding to that need. I invite you to be understanding, compassionate, and still offer wisdom!

day 12

"Great things never came from comfort zones."

today's date: _____

Mindfulness: *Object Naming.* Set a timer for one minute. Look all around you, and in your mind, list everything you see. Try to remain non-judgmental, meaning not adding any qualitative words to the objects you see. After the minute is up, jot down what the experience was like for you in the space below.

Gratitude: *What's In Front of You.* List six things you can see, touch, hear, or notice right around you that you are grateful for.

Affirmations: *Value.* Make six affirmations about how you add value to this world.

Power Mantras for Your Abilities: Write two power mantras about your abilities.

day 13

"Comparison isn't the only thief of joy, it's also the thief of dreams."
-Theodore Roosevelt

Mindfulness: *Object Naming.* Set a timer for one minute. Look all around you, and in your mind, list everything you see. Try to remain non-judgmental, meaning not adding any qualitative words to the objects you see. After the minute is up, jot down what the experience was like for you in the space below.

Gratitude: *This Past Month.* List six things you are grateful for from this past month.

Affirmations: Complete the following affirmations:

I am:

I have a beautiful:

I excel at:

I love my:

I am really good at:

I am skilled at:

Exponential Manifestation Statements: Think of something you'd like to accomplish in the next year. Get specific. Use the SAME GOAL for all three statements: they are each more powerful than the previous.
In the next year, I want to...

In the next year I will...

By the end of this year, I will...

day 14

"It's okay if you fall apart sometimes. Tacos fall apart and we still love them."

today's date: _____

starting mood: _____

ending mood: _____

Mindfulness: *Object Observation.* Set a timer for one minute. Choose an object in your line of sight. Using "beginner's mind," try to remain non-judgmental, meaning not adding any qualitative words to the observations you make. When the timer goes off, jot down what the experience was like for you.

Gratitude: *Material items.* List six material items you are grateful for and why.

Affirmations: *What You Attract.* Make six affirmations about positive experiences, material items, or relationships you attract.

Month Ahead Manifestations: Think of something specific you hope to achieve. Maybe it's a dream you've had for a long time. Maybe it's a new goal you're working towards. Make statements like, "I will," or "I am going to," rather than "I hope to," or "I want to." Be specific with timing and words. Write it down in the space below. Say it out loud three times to really send it out into the universe.

day 15

*"Remember you were once a toddler who strutted with
her belly forward."*

today's date: _____

Mindfulness: *Free Doodle.* Set a timer for one minute. Doodle in the space provided. If your thoughts wander or if you notice yourself starting to make judgments about your doodling, simply notice those thoughts and return your attention to your drawing.

Gratitude: *Life Right Now.* List six things you are grateful for in your life right now.

Affirmations: *Talents and Skills. Make six affirmations about your talents and skills.*

Manifestation Statement: Make one, powerful statement about what you hope to manifest for your self-worth. Write it three times, each time making the words bigger on the page.

day 16

"Seek to be whole, not perfect."
-Oprah

starting mood: _____

today's date: _____   ending mood: _____

Mindfulness: *Connect the Dots.* Starting from the left of the box below, connect the dots from left to right without lifting your pen from the page. You can draw up, down, diagonally, backward, and forward. Try to focus on each dot as you connect them. If your thoughts wander or if you notice yourself starting to make judgments, simply notice those thoughts and return to connecting the dots.

• •
• •
• •
• •

Gratitude: *Lessons Learned.* Think of three lessons you have learned this year that you are grateful for, and why.

Affirmations: Complete the following affirmations:

I am:

I have a beautiful:

I excel at:

I love my:

I am really good at:

I am skilled at:

Power Mantras for Letting Go: Write two power mantras that have to do with surrender, letting go, and radical acceptance.

day 17

"The way to walk in freedom is to surrender control."

Mindfulness: *Object Naming.* Set a timer for one minute. Look all around you, and in your mind, list everything you see. Try to remain non-judgmental, meaning not adding any qualitative words to the objects you see. After the minute is up, jot down what the experience was like for you in the space below.

Gratitude: *This Past Month.* List six things you are grateful for from this past month.

Affirmations: *Freebie.* Make your own category or prompts for what you will write affirmations about and write four affirmations based on that category below.

Expectations

Mini-Mantras

day 18

"Don't feel guilty doing what is best for you."
-Hannah Neese

starting mood: _____

today's date: _____

ending mood: _____

Mindfulness: *Sound Observation.* Set a timer for one minute. Close your eyes. Listen to all the sounds around you. Try to remain non-judgmental, meaning not adding any qualitative words to the sounds you hear. When the timer goes off, jot down what the experience was like for you.

Gratitude: *Something You're Not Grateful for.* Find four things you are grateful for in regards to a specific thing you are presently feeling ungrateful for.

Affirmations: *From Another.* Write five affirmations that you would fill your heart if a parent, caregiver, or idol said them to you.

Power Mantras for Your Worth: Write two power mantras about your worthiness as a human being.

day 19

"Sometimes, it's not the times you decide to fight, but the times you decide to surrender that make all the difference."
-Sissy Gavrilaki

starting mood: _____

today's date: _____   ending mood: _____

Mindfulness: *Energy Ball.* Sit in a comfortable position with your legs and arms uncrossed, eyes closed. Starting with your toes, imagine a warm ball of energy moving up your body. Once the energy ball reaches the top of your head, return it to your third eye center (the space between your eyebrows). Imagine the ball of energy and visualize what color it is. Jot down what the experience was like in the space below.

Gratitude: *Freebie.* Make your own category or prompts for what you will write gratitude statements about and make four gratitude statements below!

Affirmations: *Talents and Skills.* Make six affirmations about your talents and skills.

Month Ahead Manifestations: Think of something specific you hope to achieve. Maybe it's a dream you've had for a long time. Maybe it's a new goal you're working towards. Make statements like, "I will," or "I am going to," rather than "I hope to," or "I want to." Be specific with timing and words. Write it down in the space below. Say it out loud three times to really send it out into the universe.

day 20

"Self-care is not an expense, it's an investment."

Mindfulness: *Body Scan.* Sit in a comfortable position with your legs and arms uncrossed, eyes closed. Starting with your toes, visualize each part of your body until you reach the top of your head. Visualize your joints, muscles, anything that comes to mind. If your thoughts wander or if you notice yourself starting to make judgments about your body parts, simply notice those thoughts and gently return to the body part you are on. Jot down what the experience was like in the space below.

Gratitude: *Self.* List six things you are grateful for in yourself.

Affirmations: *Appearance.* Make six affirmations about your appearance.

Power Mantras for Wisdom: Write two power mantras about your inner wisdom.

day 21

"If something goes wrong in your life, just yell, plot twist!
And move on."

starting mood: _____

today's date: _____   ending mood: _____

Letter to Yourself: *Inner Child*: Picture yourself as a little kid. Pick a specific age. For me, I generally choose 3-4 years old. Visualize yourself. If you have an old photo, pull it out and look at it. What do you want to say to that little person? Write down what you come up with.

day 22

"To pay attention, this is our endless and proper work."
-Mary Oliver

Mindfulness: *Object Sensory Observation.* Set a timer for one minute. Pick up an object near you and close your eyes. Using "beginner's mind," imagine you are feeling this object for the first time. After the minute is up, jot down what the experience was like for you in the space below.

Gratitude: *Abilities.* List six abilities you have that you are grateful for and why.

Affirmations: *Worth.* Make six affirmations about your worth.

Manifestation Statement: Make one, powerful statement about what you hope to manifest for your self-worth. Write it three times, each time making the words bigger on the page.

day 23

"Visualize your highest self and start showing up as her."

Mindfulness: *Object Observation.* Set a timer for one minute. Choose an object in your line of sight. Using "beginner's mind," try to remain non-judgmental, meaning not adding any qualitative words to the observations you make. When the timer goes off, jot down what the experience was like for you.

Gratitude: List four opportunities you have had or are going to have that you are grateful for.

Affirmations: *Freebie.* Make your own category or prompts for what you will write affirmations about and write four affirmations based on that category below.

Power Mantras for Your Abilities: Write two power mantras about your abilities.

day 24

"Flowers need time to bloom. So do you."
-Sajid Al Sayed

starting mood: _____

today's date: _____   ending mood: _____

Mindfulness: *Pen-to-Page Doodle.* Set a timer for one minute. Doodle in the space provided without lifting your pen from the page. If your thoughts wander or if you notice yourself starting to make judgments about your doodling, simply notice those thoughts and return your attention to your pen on the page.

Gratitude: *This Past Month.* List six things you are grateful for from this past month.

Affirmations: *Talents and Skills.* Make six affirmations about your talents and skills.

Expectations   **Mini-Mantras**

day 25

"Doubt kills more dreams than failure ever will."
-Suzy Kassem

today's date: _____

Mindfulness: *Free Doodle.* Set a timer for one minute. Doodle in the space provided. If your thoughts wander or if you notice yourself starting to make judgments about your doodling, simply notice those thoughts and return your attention to your drawing.

Gratitude: *What's In Front of You.* List six things you can see, touch, hear, or notice right around you that you are grateful for.

Affirmations: *From Another.* Write five affirmations that you would fill your heart if a parent, caregiver, or idol said them to you.

Power Mantras for Letting Go: Write two power mantras that have to do with surrender, letting go, and radical acceptance.

day 26

"One day you will tell your story of how you overcame what you went through and it will be someone else's survival guide."
-Brene Brown

today's date: _____

starting mood: _____

ending mood: _____

Mindfulness: *Object Naming.* Set a timer for one minute. Look all around you, and in your mind, list everything you see. Try to remain non-judgmental, meaning not adding any qualitative words to the objects you see. After the minute is up, jot down what the experience was like for you in the space below.

Gratitude: *Yesterday.* List four things you are grateful for from yesterday.

Affirmations: *Value.* Make six affirmations about how you add value to this world.

Manifestation Statement: Make one, powerful statement about what you hope to manifest for your self-worth. Write it three times, each time making the words bigger on the page.

day 27

"The more you let go, the higher you rise."
-Yasmin Mogahed

starting mood: _____

today's date: _____   ending mood: _____

Mindfulness: *Object Sensory Observation.* Set a timer for one minute. Pick up an object near you and close your eyes. Using "beginner's mind," imagine you are feeling this object for the first time. After the minute is up, jot down what the experience was like for you in the space below.

Gratitude: *Material items.* List six material items you are grateful for and why.

Affirmations: *Worth.* Make six affirmations about your worth.

Month Ahead Manifestations: Think of something specific you hope to achieve. Maybe it's a dream you've had for a long time. Maybe it's a new goal you're working towards. Make statements like, "I will," or "I am going to," rather than "I hope to," or "I want to." Be specific with timing and words. Write it down in the space below. Say it out loud three times to really send it out into the universe.

day 28

"When we are no longer able to change a situation, we are challenged to change ourselves."
-Viktor Frankl

starting mood: _____

today's date: _____   ending mood: _____

Mindfulness: *Pen-to-Page Doodle.* Set a timer for one minute. Doodle in the space provided without lifting your pen from the page. If your thoughts wander or if you notice yourself starting to make judgments about your doodling, simply notice those thoughts and return your attention to your pen on the page.

Gratitude: *Lessons Learned.* Think of three lessons you have learned this year that you are grateful for, and why.

Affirmations: *What You Have Power Over.* Write six affirmations about what you have power of, when you are powerful, or why you have power.

Power Mantras for Your Worth: Write two power mantras about your worth.

day 29

"Trust the timing of your life."
-Brittany Burgunder

today's date: _____

Mindfulness: *Sound Observation.* Set a timer for one minute. Close your eyes. Listen to all the sounds around you. Try to remain non-judgmental, meaning not adding any qualitative words to the sounds you hear. When the timer goes off, jot down what the experience was like for you.

Gratitude: *Relationships.* List six people you are grateful for, and why.

Affirmations: *What You Attract.* Make six affirmations about positive experiences, material items, or relationships you attract.

Power Mantras for Your Abilities: Write two power mantras about your abilities.

day 30

"Don't compare your life to others. There's no comparison between the sun and the moon, they shine when it's their time."
-Stephanie H. Brown

Mindfulness: *Connect the Dots.* Starting from the left of the box below, connect the dots from left to right without lifting your pen from the page. You can draw up, down, diagonally, backward, and forward. Try to focus on each dot as you connect them. If your thoughts wander or if you notice yourself starting to make judgments, simply notice those thoughts and return to connecting the dots.

. . . .
. . . .
. . . .
. . . .

Gratitude: *This Past Month.* List six things you are grateful for from this past month.

Affirmations: *Freebie.* Make your own category or prompts for what you will write affirmations about and write four affirmations based on that category below.

Expectations   **Mini-Mantras**

you've journaled for 30 days!

take a moment
to reflect

Reflection is one of the biggest indicators of future success. It allows us to see where we started, how we've grown, and teaches our brains that we are adaptable and flexible beings.

In the space below, free-write about the last month. What did you learn? What was challenging? How have you grown? What would you like to tell yourself as the next 30 days unfold?

day 31

"A mind is like a parachute. It doesn't work if it isn't open."
-Frank Zappa

starting mood: _____

today's date: _____   ending mood: _____

Letter to Yourself: *You Matter:* Imagine you are a close friend or family member. Choose someone who knows you well and is kind. From their perspective, write a letter to yourself about why you matter.

day 32

"When you focus on the good, the good gets better."
-Abraham Hicks

starting mood: _____

today's date: _____   ending mood: _____

Mindfulness: *Object Observation.* Set a timer for one minute. Choose an object in your line of sight. Using "beginner's mind," try to remain non-judgmental, meaning not adding any qualitative words to the observations you make. When the timer goes off, jot down what the experience was like for you.

Gratitude: *Yesterday.* List four things you are grateful for from yesterday.

Affirmations: *Worth.* Make six affirmations about your worth.

Power Mantras for Wisdom: Write two power mantras about your inner wisdom. abilities.

day 33

"I exist as I am, that is enough."
-Walt Whitman

starting mood: _____

today's date: _____

ending mood: _____

Mindfulness: *Pen-to-Page Doodle.* Set a timer for one minute. Doodle in the space provided without lifting your pen from the page. If your thoughts wander or if you notice yourself starting to make judgments about your doodling, simply notice those thoughts and return your attention to your pen on the page.

Gratitude: *Life Right Now.* List six things you are grateful for in your life right now.

Affirmations: Complete the following affirmations:

I am:

I have a beautiful:

I excel at:

I love my:

I am really good at:

I am skilled at:

Expectations

Mini-Mantras

day 34

"Be yourself. Everyone else is already taken."
-Oscar Wilde

starting mood: _____

today's date: _____

ending mood: _____

Mindfulness: *Free Doodle*. Set a timer for one minute. Doodle in the space provided. If your thoughts wander or if you notice yourself starting to make judgments about your doodling, simply notice those thoughts and return your attention to your drawing.

Gratitude: *Abilities*. List six abilities you have that you are grateful for and why.

Affirmations: *Personality*. Make six affirmations about your personality.

Power Mantras for Your Abilities: Write two power mantras about your abilities.

day 35

"Be brave enough to be bad at something new."
–Jon Acuff

Mindfulness: *Energy Ball.* Sit in a comfortable position with your legs and arms uncrossed, eyes closed. Starting with your toes, imagine a warm ball of energy moving up your body. Once the energy ball reaches the top of your head, return it to your third eye center (the space between your eyebrows). Imagine the ball of energy and visualize what color it is. Jot down what the experience was like in the space below.

Gratitude: *Occupation.* Think of four things you are grateful for about your job, school, retirement, or unemployment.

Affirmations: *Freebie.* Make your own category or prompts for what you will write affirmations about and write four affirmations based on that category below.

Month Ahead Manifestations: Think of something specific you hope to achieve. Maybe it's a dream you've had for a long time. Maybe it's a new goal you're working towards. Make statements like, "I will," or "I am going to," rather than "I hope to," or "I want to." Be specific with timing and words. Write it down in the space below. Say it out loud three times to really send it out into the universe.

day 36

"When joy is a habit, love is a reflex."
-Bob Goff

today's date: _____

Mindfulness: *Object Naming.* Set a timer for one minute. Look all around you, and in your mind, list everything you see. Try to remain non-judgmental, meaning not adding any qualitative words to the objects you see. After the minute is up, jot down what the experience was like for you in the space below.

Gratitude: *Events.* Pick a past or future event, and think of six things you are grateful for regarding the event.

Affirmations: *Talents and Skills.* Make six affirmations about your talents and skills.

Expectations   **Mini-Mantras**

day 37

*"Being positive in a negative situation is not naive.
It's leadership."*
-Ralph Marston

Mindfulness: *Sound Observation.* Set a timer for one minute. Close your eyes. Listen to all the sounds around you. Try to remain non-judgmental, meaning not adding any qualitative words to the sounds you hear. When the timer goes off, jot down what the experience was like for you.

Gratitude: *Lessons Learned.* Think of three lessons you have learned this year that you are grateful for, and why.

Affirmations: *Appearance.* Make six affirmations about your appearance.

Power Mantras for Wisdom: Write two power mantras about your inner wisdom.

day 38

"Authenticity is the daily practice of letting go of who we think we're supposed to be and embracing who we are."
-Brene Brown

Mindfulness: *Object Sensory Observation*. Set a timer for one minute. Pick up an object near you and close your eyes. Using "beginner's mind," imagine you are feeling this object for the first time. After the minute is up, jot down what the experience was like for you in the space below.

Gratitude: *Freebie*. Make your own category or prompts for what you will write gratitude statements about and make four gratitude statements below!

Affirmations: *From Another*. Write five affirmations that you would fill your heart if a parent, caregiver, or idol said them to you.

Month Ahead Manifestations: Think of something specific you hope to achieve. Maybe it's a dream you've had for a long time. Maybe it's a new goal you're working towards. Make statements like, "I will," or "I am going to," rather than "I hope to," or "I want to." Be specific with timing and words. Write it down in the space below. Say it out loud three times to really send it out into the universe.

day 39

"You are the artist of your own life. Don't hand the paintbrush to anyone else."
-Iva Ursano

starting mood: _____

today's date: _____   ending mood: _____

Mindfulness: *Body Scan.* Sit in a comfortable position with your legs and arms uncrossed, eyes closed. Starting with your toes, visualize each part of your body until you reach the top of your head. Visualize your joints, muscles, anything that comes to mind. If your thoughts wander or if you notice yourself starting to make judgments about your body parts, simply notice those thoughts and gently return to the body part you are on. Jot down what the experience was like in the space below.

Gratitude: *What's In Front of You.* List six things you can see, touch, hear, or notice right around you that you are grateful for.

Affirmations: *What You Have Power Over.* Write six affirmations about what you have power of, when you are powerful, or why you have power.

Manifestation Statement: Make one, powerful statement about what you hope to manifest for your self-worth. Write it three times, each time making the words bigger on the page.

day 40

"You have so much to offer as the person you are right now."
-Robyn Conley Downs

starting mood: _____

today's date: _____   ending mood: _____

Mindfulness: *Pen-to-Page Doodle.* Set a timer for one minute. Doodle in the space provided without lifting your pen from the page. If your thoughts wander or if you notice yourself starting to make judgments about your doodling, simply notice those thoughts and return your attention to your pen on the page.

Gratitude: *Something You're Not Grateful for.* Find four things you are grateful for in regards to a specific thing you are presently feeling ungrateful for.

Affirmations: *When you Shine.* Write six affirmations about times you really shine!

Exponential Manifestation Statements: Think of something you'd like to accomplish in the next year. Get specific. Use the SAME GOAL for all three statements: they are each more powerful than the previous.
In the next year, I want to...

In the next year I will...

By the end of this year, I will...

day 41

"How you love yourself is how you teach others to love you."
-Rupi Kaur

starting mood: _____

today's date: _____   ending mood: _____

Letter to Yourself: What Do I Need to Hear? Ask yourself, "what do I need right now?" Write the answer at the top of the page, then write yourself a letter responding to that need. I invite you to be understanding, compassionate, and still offer wisdom!

day 42

"Feel what you need to feel and then let it go. Do not let it consume you."
-Dhiman

starting mood: _____

today's date: _____

ending mood: _____

Mindfulness: *Object Naming. Set a timer for one minute. Look all around you, and in your mind, list everything you see. Try to remain non-judgmental, meaning not adding any qualitative words to the objects you see. After the minute is up, jot down what the experience was like for you in the space below.*

Gratitude: *Self.* List six things you are grateful for in yourself.

Affirmations: *Personality.* Make six affirmations about your personality.

Expectations

Mini-Mantras

day 43

"I hope you live a life you're proud of. If you find that you are not, I hope you have the strength to start all over again."
-F. Scott Fitzgerald

starting mood: _____

today's date: _____   ending mood: _____

Mindfulness: *Free Doodle.* Set a timer for one minute. Doodle in the space provided. If your thoughts wander or if you notice yourself starting to make judgments about your doodling, simply notice those thoughts and return your attention to your drawing.

Gratitude: *Opportunities.* List four opportunities you have had or are going to have that you are grateful for.

Affirmations: *Talents and Skills.* Make six affirmations about your talents and skills.

Power Mantras for Your Abilities: Write two power mantras about your abilities.

day 44

"You don't have to control your thoughts. You just have to stop letting them control you."
-Dan Millman

starting mood: _____

today's date: _____ ending mood: _____

Mindfulness: *Energy Ball.* Sit in a comfortable position with your legs and arms uncrossed, eyes closed. Starting with your toes, imagine a warm ball of energy moving up your body. Once the energy ball reaches the top of your head, return it to your third eye center (the space between your eyebrows). Imagine the ball of energy and visualize what color it is. Jot down what the experience was like in the space below.

Gratitude: *Occupation.* Think of four things you are grateful for about your job, school, retirement, or unemployment.

Affirmations: *Freebie.* Make your own category or prompts for what you will write affirmations about and write four affirmations based on that category below.

Month Ahead Manifestations: Think of something specific you hope to achieve. Maybe it's a dream you've had for a long time. Maybe it's a new goal you're working towards. Make statements like, "I will," or "I am going to," rather than "I hope to," or "I want to." Be specific with timing and words. Write it down in the space below. Say it out loud three times to really send it out into the universe.

day 45

"Mindfulness: the intentional use of attention."
-Leah Weiss

Mindfulness: *Object Observation.* Set a timer for one minute. Choose an object in your line of sight. Using "beginner's mind," try to remain non-judgmental, meaning not adding any qualitative words to the observations you make. When the timer goes off, jot down what the experience was like for you.

Gratitude: *Yesterday.* List four things you are grateful for from yesterday.

Affirmations: *From Another.* Write five affirmations that you would fill your heart if a parent, caregiver, or idol said them to you.

Exponential Manifestation Statements: Think of something you'd like to accomplish in the next year. Get specific. Use the SAME GOAL for all three statements: they are each more powerful than the previous.
In the next year, I want to...

In the next year I will...

By the end of this year, I will...

day 46

"Your future needs you. Your past doesn't."

Mindfulness: *Sound Observation.* Set a timer for one minute. Close your eyes. Listen to all the sounds around you. Try to remain non-judgmental, meaning not adding any qualitative words to the sounds you hear. When the timer goes off, jot down what the experience was like for you.

Gratitude: *Abilities.* List six abilities you have that you are grateful for and why.

Affirmations: *What You Have Power Over.* Write six affirmations about what you have power of, when you are powerful, or why you have power.

Power Mantras for Letting Go: Write two power mantras that have to do with surrender, letting go, and radical acceptance.

day 47

"Trust the wait. Embrace the uncertainty. Enjoy the beauty of becoming."

today's date: _____

Mindfulness: *Object Sensory Observation.* Set a timer for one minute. Pick up an object near you and close your eyes. Using "beginner's mind," imagine you are feeling this object for the first time. After the minute is up, jot down what the experience was like for you in the space below.

Gratitude: *This Past Year.* List six things you are grateful for from this past year.

Affirmations: *What You Attract.* Make six affirmations about positive experiences, material items, or relationships you attract.

Expectations

Mini-Mantras

day 48

"Bravery is the audacity to be unhindered by failures, and to walk with freedom, strength, and hope, in the face of things unknown."
-Morgan Harper Nichols

starting mood: _____

today's date: _____   ending mood: _____

Mindfulness: *Energy Ball.* Sit in a comfortable position with your legs and arms uncrossed, eyes closed. Starting with your toes, imagine a warm ball of energy moving up your body. Once the energy ball reaches the top of your head, return it to your third eye center (the space between your eyebrows). Imagine the ball of energy and visualize what color it is. Jot down what the experience was like in the space below.

Gratitude: *Events.* Pick a past or future event, and think of six things you are grateful for regarding the event.

Affirmations: *Value.* Make six affirmations about how you add value to this world.

Power Mantras for Wisdom: Write two power mantras about your inner wisdom.

day 49

"Ask for what you want and be prepared to get it."
-Maya Angelou

starting mood: _____

today's date: _____   ending mood: _____

Mindfulness: *Pen-to-Page Doodle.* Set a timer for one minute. Doodle in the space provided without lifting your pen from the page. If your thoughts wander or if you notice yourself starting to make judgments about your doodling, simply notice those thoughts and return your attention to your pen on the page.

Gratitude: *Variety Pack.* List what you are grateful for in the following six categories:

Nature

Material items

Self

Relationships

Food

General

Affirmations: *From Another.* Write five affirmations that you would fill your heart if a parent, caregiver, or idol said them to you.

Manifestation Statement: Make one, powerful statement about what you hope to manifest for your self-worth. Write it three times, each time making the words bigger on the page.

day 50

"When you feel like quitting, think about why you started."

Mindfulness: *Body Scan.* Sit in a comfortable position with your legs and arms uncrossed, eyes closed. Starting with your toes, visualize each part of your body until you reach the top of your head. Visualize your joints, muscles, anything that comes to mind. If your thoughts wander or if you notice yourself starting to make judgments about your body parts, simply notice those thoughts and gently return to the body part you are on. Jot down what the experience was like in the space below.

Gratitude: *Self.* List six things you are grateful for in yourself.

Affirmations: *Complete the following affirmations:*

I am:

I have a beautiful:

I excel at:

I love my:

I am really good at:

I am skilled at:

Power Mantras for Letting Go: Write two power mantras that have to do with surrender, letting go, and radical acceptance.

day 51

You change the world by being yourself."
-Yoko Ono

starting mood: _____

today's date: _____

ending mood: _____

Letter to Yourself: *Inner Child.* Picture yourself as a little kid. Pick a specific age. For me, I generally choose 3-4 years old. Visualize yourself. If you have an old photo, pull it out and look at it. What do you want to say to that little person? Write down what you come up with.

day 52

"It's ok. You just forgot who you are. Welcome back."

starting mood: _____

today's date: _____   ending mood: _____

Mindfulness: *Free Doodle.* Set a timer for one minute. Doodle in the space provided. If your thoughts wander or if you notice yourself starting to make judgments about your doodling, simply notice those thoughts and return your attention to your drawing.

Gratitude: *Lessons Learned.* Think of three lessons you have learned this year that you are grateful for, and why.

Affirmations: *Talents and Skills.* Make four affirmations about your talents and skills.

Expectations   **Mini-Mantras**

day 53

"If you feel like you're losing everything, remember that trees lose their leaves every year and still they stand tall and wait for better days to come."

today's date: _____

starting mood: _____

ending mood: _____

Mindfulness: *Connect the Dots.* Starting from the left of the box below, connect the dots from left to right without lifting your pen from the page. You can draw up, down, diagonally, backward, and forward. Try to focus on each dot as you connect them. If your thoughts wander or if you notice yourself starting to make judgments, simply notice those thoughts and return to connecting the dots.

· ·
· ·
· ·
· ·

Gratitude: *Material items.* List six material items you are grateful for and why.

Affirmations: *Freebie.* Make your own category or prompts for what you will write affirmations about and write four affirmations based on that category below.

Power Mantras for Wisdom: Write two power mantras about your inner wisdom.

day 54

"You carry so much love in your heart.
Give some to yourself."

Mindfulness: *Object Naming.* Set a timer for one minute. Look all around you, and in your mind, list everything you see. Try to remain non-judgmental, meaning not adding any qualitative words to the objects you see. After the minute is up, jot down what the experience was like for you in the space below.

Gratitude: *This Past Month.* List six things you are grateful for from this past month.

Affirmations: *Personality.* Make six affirmations about your personality.

Exponential Manifestation Statements: Think of something you'd like to accomplish in the next year. Get specific. Use the SAME GOAL for all three statements: they are each more powerful than the previous.
In the next year, I want to...

In the next year I will...

By the end of this year, I will...

day 55

"The wound is the place where the light enters you."
-Rumi

starting mood: _____

today's date: _____   ending mood: _____

Mindfulness: *Object Sensory Observation.* Set a timer for one minute. Pick up an object near you and close your eyes. Using "beginner's mind," imagine you are feeling this object for the first time. After the minute is up, jot down what the experience was like for you in the space below.

Gratitude: *Self.* List six things you are grateful for in yourself.

Affirmations: *What You Have Power Over.* Write six affirmations about what you have power of, when you are powerful, or why you have power.

Manifestation Statement: Make one, powerful statement about what you hope to manifest for your self-worth. Write it three times, each time making the words bigger on the page.

day 56

"Rock bottom will teach you lessons that mountain tops never will."
-Michelle Hannah Ministries

Mindfulness: *Energy Ball.* Sit in a comfortable position with your legs and arms uncrossed, eyes closed. Starting with your toes, imagine a warm ball of energy moving up your body. Once the energy ball reaches the top of your head, return it to your third eye center (the space between your eyebrows). Imagine the ball of energy and visualize what color it is. Jot down what the experience was like in the space below.

Gratitude: *Yesterday.* List four things you are grateful for from yesterday.

Affirmations: *Complete the following affirmations:*

I am:

I have a beautiful:

I excel at:

I love my:

I am really good at:

I am skilled at:

Power Mantras for Your Worth: Write two power mantras about your worthiness as a human being.

day 57

""Daring is saying I know I will eventually fail and I'm still all in."
-Brene Brown

starting mood: _____

today's date: _____   ending mood: _____

Mindfulness: *Sound Observation.* Set a timer for one minute. Close your eyes. Listen to all the sounds around you. Try to remain non-judgmental, meaning not adding any qualitative words to the sounds you hear. When the timer goes off, jot down what the experience was like for you.

Gratitude: *Life Right Now.* List six things you are grateful for in your life right now.

Affirmations: *Freebie.* Make your own category or prompts for what you will write affirmations about, and write four affirmations based on that category below.

Month Ahead Manifestations: Think of something specific you hope to achieve. Maybe it's a dream you've had for a long time. Maybe it's a new goal you're working towards. Make statements like, "I will," or "I am going to," rather than "I hope to," or "I want to." Be specific with timing and words. Write it down in the space below. Say it out loud three times to really send it out into the universe.

day 58

"But even if I am weak, I can still be kind. For true power is in giving instead of taking."

Mindfulness: *Body Scan.* Sit in a comfortable position with your legs and arms uncrossed, eyes closed. Starting with your toes, visualize each part of your body until you reach the top of your head. Visualize your joints, muscles, anything that comes to mind. If your thoughts wander or if you notice yourself starting to make judgments about your body parts, simply notice those thoughts and gently return to the body part you are on. Jot down what the experience was like in the space below.

Gratitude: *Relationships.* List six people you are grateful for, and why.

Affirmations: *Worth.* Make six affirmations about your worth.

Power Mantras for Your Abilities: Write two power mantras about your abilities.

day 59

"If you get tired, learn to rest, not to quit."
-Banksy

starting mood: _____

today's date: _____   ending mood: _____

Mindfulness: *Object Observation.* Set a timer for one minute. Choose an object in your line of sight. Using "beginner's mind," try to remain non-judgmental, meaning not adding any qualitative words to the observations you make. When the timer goes off, jot down what the experience was like for you.

Gratitude: *Self.* List six things you are grateful for in yourself.

Affirmations: *From Another.* Write five affirmations that you would fill your heart if a parent, caregiver, or idol said them to you.

Manifestation Statement: Make one, powerful statement about what you hope to manifest for your self-worth. Write it three times, each time making the words bigger on the page.

day 60

"If you don't like where you are, move. You are not a tree."
–Jim Rohn

starting mood: _____

today's date: _____   ending mood: _____

Mindfulness: *Object Sensory Observation.* Set a timer for one minute. Pick up an object near you and close your eyes. Using "beginner's mind," imagine you are feeling this object for the first time. After the minute is up, jot down what the experience was like for you in the space below.

Gratitude: *Abilities.* List six abilities you have that you are grateful for and why.

Affirmations: *Talents and Skills.* Make six affirmations about your talents and skills.

Power Mantras for Letting Go: Write two power mantras that have to do with surrender, letting go, and radical acceptance.

you've journaled for 60 days!

take a moment
to reflect

Reflection is one of the biggest indicators of future success. It allows us to see where we started, how we've grown, and teaches our brains that we are adaptable and flexible beings.

In the space below, free-write about the last month. What did you learn? What was challenging? How have you grown? What would you like to tell yourself as the next 30 days unfold?

day 61

"Even the darkest night will end and the sun will rise."
-Victor Hugo

today's date: _____

Letter to Yourself: *You Matter.* Imagine you are a close friend or family member. Choose someone who knows you well and is kind. From their perspective, write a letter to yourself about why you matter.

day 62

"When someone says you can't do it, do it twice, and take pictures."
-Tami Xiang

starting mood: _____

today's date: _____   ending mood: _____

Mindfulness: *Body Scan.* Sit in a comfortable position with your legs and arms uncrossed, eyes closed. Starting with your toes, visualize each part of your body until you reach the top of your head. Visualize your joints, muscles, anything that comes to mind. If your thoughts wander or if you notice yourself starting to make judgments about your body parts, simply notice those thoughts and gently return to the body part you are on. Jot down what the experience was like in the space below.

Gratitude: *Yesterday. List four things you are grateful for from yesterday.*

Affirmations: Complete the following affirmations:

I am:

I have a beautiful:

I excel at:

I love my:

I am really good at:

I am skilled at:

Power Mantras for Your Worth: Write two power mantras about your worthiness as a human being.

day 63

*"Your anxiety doesn't come from thinking about the future,
but from wanting to control it."*
-Kahlil Girban

starting mood: _____

today's date: _____   ending mood: _____

Mindfulness: *Energy Ball.* Sit in a comfortable position with your legs and arms uncrossed, eyes closed. Starting with your toes, imagine a warm ball of energy moving up your body. Once the energy ball reaches the top of your head, return it to your third eye center (the space between your eyebrows). Imagine the ball of energy and visualize what color it is. Jot down what the experience was like in the space below.

Gratitude: *Occupation.* Think of four things you are grateful for about your job, school, retirement, or unemployment.

Affirmations: *Talents and Skills.* Make six affirmations about your talents and skills.

Expectations   **Mini-Mantras**

day 64

""The wars inside my head don't define me."

starting mood: _____

today's date: _____   ending mood: _____

Mindfulness: *Object Naming.* Set a timer for one minute. Look all around you, and in your mind, list everything you see. Try to remain non-judgmental, meaning not adding any qualitative words to the objects you see. After the minute is up, jot down what the experience was like for you in the space below.

Gratitude: *Freebie.* Make your own category or prompts for what you will write gratitude statements about and make four gratitude statements below!

Affirmations: *Appearance.* Make six affirmations about your appearance.

Month Ahead Manifestations: Think of something specific you hope to achieve. Maybe it's a dream you've had for a long time. Maybe it's a new goal you're working towards. Make statements like, "I will," or "I am going to," rather than "I hope to," or "I want to." Be specific with timing and words. Write it down in the space below. Say it out loud three times to really send it out into the universe.

day 65

"You are not a drop in the ocean. You are the entire ocean in a drop."
-Rumi

Mindfulness: *Sound Observation.* Set a timer for one minute. Close your eyes. Listen to all the sounds around you. Try to remain non-judgmental, meaning not adding any qualitative words to the sounds you hear. When the timer goes off, jot down what the experience was like for you.

Gratitude: *Variety Pack.* List what you are grateful for in the following six categories:

Nature

Material items

Self

Relationships

Food

General

Affirmations: *Value.* Make six affirmations about how you add value to this world:

Manifestation Statement: Make one, powerful statement about what you hope to manifest for your self-worth. Write it three times, each time making the words bigger on the page.

day 66

"I don't want to end up simply having visited this world."
-Mary Oliver

starting mood: _____

today's date: _____   ending mood: _____

Mindfulness: *Object Sensory Observation*. Set a timer for one minute. Pick up an object near you and close your eyes. Using "beginner's mind," imagine you are feeling this object for the first time. After the minute is up, jot down what the experience was like for you in the space below.

Gratitude: *This Past Year*. List six things you are grateful for from this past year.

Affirmations: *When you Shine*. Write six affirmations about times you really shine!

Power Mantras for Letting Go: Write two power mantras that have to do with surrender, letting go, and radical acceptance.

day 67

"I am not what happened to me, I am what I choose to become."
-Carl Jung

today's date: _____

Mindfulness: *Connect the Dots.* Starting from the left of the box below, connect the dots from left to right without lifting your pen from the page. You can draw up, down, diagonally, backward, and forward. Try to focus on each dot as you connect them. If your thoughts wander or if you notice yourself starting to make judgments, simply notice those thoughts and return to connecting the dots.

• •
• •
• •
• •

Gratitude: *Something You're Not Grateful for.* Find four things you are grateful for in regards to a specific thing you are presently feeling ungrateful for.

Affirmations: *What You Have Power Over.* Write six affirmations about what you have power of, when you are powerful, or why you have power.

Exponential Manifestation Statements: Think of something you'd like to accomplish in the next year. Get specific. Use the SAME GOAL for all three statements: they are each more powerful than the previous.
In the next year, I want to...

In the next year I will...

By the end of this year, I will...

day 68

"Having compassion for yourself and your body comes from embracing your humanness."

Mindfulness: *Energy Ball.* Sit in a comfortable position with your legs and arms uncrossed, eyes closed. Starting with your toes, imagine a warm ball of energy moving up your body. Once the energy ball reaches the top of your head, return it to your third eye center (the space between your eyebrows). Imagine the ball of energy and visualize what color it is. Jot down what the experience was like in the space below.

Gratitude: *Self.* List six things you are grateful for in yourself.

Affirmations: *Personality.* Make six affirmations about your personality.

Power Mantras for Wisdom: Write two power mantras about your inner wisdom.

day 69

"When you become comfortable with uncertainty, infinite possibilities open up in your life."
-Eckhart Tolle

starting mood: _____

today's date: _____   ending mood: _____

Mindfulness: *Free Doodle.* Set a timer for one minute. Doodle in the space provided. If your thoughts wander or if you notice yourself starting to make judgments about your doodling, simply notice those thoughts and return your attention to your drawing.

Gratitude: *Lessons Learned.* Think of three lessons you have learned this year that you are grateful for, and why.

Affirmations: *Talents and Skills.* Make six affirmations about your talents and skills.

Month Ahead Manifestations: Think of something specific you hope to achieve. Maybe it's a dream you've had for a long time. Maybe it's a new goal you're working towards. Make statements like, "I will," or "I am going to," rather than "I hope to," or "I want to." Be specific with timing and words. Write it down in the space below. Say it out loud three times to really send it out into the universe.

day 70

"When things change inside you, things change around you."
-Mark Twain

starting mood: _____

today's date: _____

ending mood: _____

Mindfulness: *Object Sensory Observation.* Set a timer for one minute. Pick up an object near you and close your eyes. Using "beginner's mind," imagine you are feeling this object for the first time. After the minute is up, jot down what the experience was like for you in the space below.

Gratitude: *This Past Year.* List six things you are grateful for from this past year.

Affirmations: *Worth.* Make six affirmations about your worth.

Manifestation Statement: Make one, powerful statement about what you hope to manifest for your self-worth. Write it three times, each time making the words bigger on the page.

day 71

*"Uncertainty is the only certainty there is, and knowing how
to live with insecurity is the only security."*
-John Allen Paulos

starting mood: _____

today's date: _____   ending mood: _____

Letter to Yourself: What Do I Need to Hear? Ask yourself, "what do I need right now?" Write the answer at the top of the page, then write yourself a letter responding to that need. I invite you to be understanding, compassionate, and still offer wisdom!

day 72

"One moment can change a day, one day can change a life,
and one life can change the world."
-Buddha

starting mood: _____

today's date: _____   ending mood: _____

Mindfulness: *Object Naming.* Set a timer for one minute. Look all around you, and in your mind, list everything you see. Try to remain non-judgmental, meaning not adding any qualitative words to the objects you see. After the minute is up, jot down what the experience was like for you in the space below.

Gratitude: *Abilities.* List six abilities you have that you are grateful for and why.

Affirmations: Complete the following affirmations:

I am:

I have a beautiful:

I excel at:

I love my:

I am really good at:

I am skilled at:

Expectations   **Mini-Mantras**

day 73

"No one can make you feel inferior without your consent."
-Eleanor Roosevelt

starting mood: _____

today's date: _____   ending mood: _____

Mindfulness: *Object Sensory Observation.* Set a timer for one minute. Pick up an object near you and close your eyes. Using "beginner's mind," imagine you are feeling this object for the first time. After the minute is up, jot down what the experience was like for you in the space below.

Gratitude: *This Past Year.* List six things you are grateful for from this past year.

Affirmations: *Worth.* Make six affirmations about your worth.

Manifestation Statement: Make one, powerful statement about what you hope to manifest for your self-worth. Write it three times, each time making the words bigger on the page.

day 74

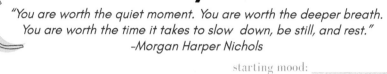

*"You are worth the quiet moment. You are worth the deeper breath.
You are worth the time it takes to slow down, be still, and rest."*
-Morgan Harper Nichols

starting mood: _____

today's date: _____   ending mood: _____

Mindfulness: *Pen-to-Page Doodle.* Set a timer for one minute. Doodle in the space provided without lifting your pen from the page. If your thoughts wander or if you notice yourself starting to make judgments about your doodling, simply notice those thoughts and return your attention to your pen on the page.

Gratitude: *Yesterday.* List four things you are grateful for from yesterday.

Affirmations: *Value.* Make six affirmations about how you add value to this world.

Power Mantras for Your Abilities: Write two power mantras about your abilities.

day 75

"Live life as if everything is rigged in your favor."
–Rumi

Mindfulness: *Connect the Dots.* Starting from the left of the box below, connect the dots from left to right without lifting your pen from the page. You can draw up, down, diagonally, backward, and forward. Try to focus on each dot as you connect them. If your thoughts wander or if you notice yourself starting to make judgments, simply notice those thoughts and return to connecting the dots.

• •
• •
• •
• •

Gratitude: *Relationships.* List six people you are grateful for, and why.

Affirmations: *From Another.* Write five affirmations that you would fill your heart if a parent, caregiver, or idol said them to you.

Month Ahead Manifestations: Think of something specific you hope to achieve. Maybe it's a dream you've had for a long time. Maybe it's a new goal you're working towards. Make statements like, "I will," or "I am going to," rather than "I hope to," or "I want to." Be specific with timing and words. Write it down in the space below. Say it out loud three times to really send it out into the universe.

day 76

"When you are confident, people become confident in you."

today's date: _____

starting mood: _____
ending mood: _____

Mindfulness: *Object Naming.* Set a timer for one minute. Look all around you, and in your mind, list everything you see. Try to remain non-judgmental, meaning not adding any qualitative words to the objects you see. After the minute is up, jot down what the experience was like for you in the space below.

Gratitude: *Self.* List six things you are grateful for in yourself.

Affirmations: *Personality.* Make six affirmations about your personality.

Manifestation Statement: Make one, powerful statement about what you hope to manifest for your self-worth. Write it three times, each time making the words bigger on the page.

day 77

Your life isn't yours if you always care what someone else thinks."
-Jade Marie

starting mood: _____

today's date: _____   ending mood: _____

Mindfulness: *Object Naming.* Set a timer for one minute. Look all around you, and in your mind, list everything you see. Try to remain non-judgmental, meaning not adding any qualitative words to the objects you see. After the minute is up, jot down what the experience was like for you in the space below.

Gratitude: *Opportunities.* List four opportunities you have had or are going to have that you are grateful for.

Affirmations: *When you Shine.* Write six affirmations about times you really shine!

Expectations   **Mini-Mantras**

day 78

"There is no joy without gratitude."
-Brene Brown

starting mood: _____

today's date: _____   ending mood: _____

Mindfulness: *Sound Observation.* Set a timer for one minute. Close your eyes. Listen to all the sounds around you. Try to remain non-judgmental, meaning not adding any qualitative words to the sounds you hear. When the timer goes off, jot down what the experience was like for you.

Gratitude: *Abilities.* List six abilities you have that you are grateful for and why.

Affirmations: *Freebie.* Make your own category or prompts for what you will write affirmations about!

Exponential Manifestation Statements: Think of something you'd like to accomplish in the next year. Get specific. Use the SAME GOAL for all three statements: they are each more powerful than the previous.
In the next year, I want to...

In the next year I will...

By the end of this year, I will...

day 79

"Be messy and complicated and afraid and show up anyway."
-Glennon Doyle

starting mood: _____

today's date: _____

ending mood: _____

Mindfulness: *Object Sensory Observation.* Set a timer for one minute. Pick up an object near you and close your eyes. Using "beginner's mind," imagine you are feeling this object for the first time. After the minute is up, jot down what the experience was like for you in the space below.

Gratitude: *Events.* Pick a past or future event, and think of six things you are grateful for regarding the event.

Affirmations: *What You Attract.* Make six affirmations about positive experiences, material items, or relationships you attract.

Manifestation Statement: Make one, powerful statement about what you hope to manifest for your self-worth. Write it three times, each time making the words bigger on the page.

day 80

"Everything comes to you at the right time. Be patient."

starting mood: _____

today's date: _____   ending mood: _____

Mindfulness: *Body Scan.* Sit in a comfortable position with your legs and arms uncrossed, eyes closed. Starting with your toes, visualize each part of your body until you reach the top of your head. Visualize your joints, muscles, anything that comes to mind. If your thoughts wander or if you notice yourself starting to make judgments about your body parts, simply notice those thoughts and gently return to the body part you are on. Jot down what the experience was like in the space below.

Gratitude: *Occupation.* Think of four things you are grateful for about your job, school, retirement, or unemployment.

Affirmations: Complete the following affirmations:

I am:

I have a beautiful:

I excel at:

I love my:

I am really good at:

I am skilled at:

Power Mantras for Your Abilities: Write two power mantras about your worthiness as a human abilities.

day 81

"Own your own story."
-Ali Edwards

Letter to Yourself: *Inner Child*. Picture yourself as a little kid. Pick a specific age. For me, I generally choose 3-4 years old. Visualize yourself. If you have an old photo, pull it out and look at it. What do you want to say to that little person? Write down what you come up with.

day 82

"Those who have a why to live can bear almost any how."
-Viktor Frankl

starting mood: _____

today's date: _____   ending mood: _____

Mindfulness: *Sound Observation.* Set a timer for one minute. Close your eyes. Listen to all the sounds around you. Try to remain non-judgmental, meaning not adding any qualitative words to the sounds you hear. When the timer goes off, jot down what the experience was like for you.

Gratitude: *Something You're Not Grateful for.* Find four things you are grateful for in regards to a specific thing you are presently feeling ungrateful for.

Affirmations: *Worth.* Make six affirmations about your worth.

Exponential Manifestation Statements: Think of something you'd like to accomplish in the next year. Get specific. Use the SAME GOAL for all three statements: they are each more powerful than the previous.
In the next year, I want to...

In the next year I will...

By the end of this year, I will...

day 83

"If your dreams don't scare you, they are too small."
-Richard Branson

today's date: _____

Mindfulness: *Object Observation.* Set a timer for one minute. Choose an object in your line of sight. Using "beginner's mind," try to remain non-judgmental, meaning not adding any qualitative words to the observations you make. When the timer goes off, jot down what the experience was like for you.

Gratitude: *Life Right Now.* List six things you are grateful for in your life right now.

Affirmations: *Freebie.* Make your own category or prompts for what you will write affirmations about!

Power Mantras for Wisdom: Write two power mantras about your inner wisdom.

day 84

"Someone is silently loving you. It's probably your mom, but still."

starting mood: _____

today's date: _____   ending mood: _____

Mindfulness: *Object Naming.* Set a timer for one minute. Look all around you, and in your mind, list everything you see. Try to remain non-judgmental, meaning not adding any qualitative words to the objects you see. After the minute is up, jot down what the experience was like for you in the space below.

Gratitude: *Variety Pack.* List what you are grateful for in the following six categories: nature, material items, self, relationships, food, general.

Affirmations: *What You Have Power Over.* Write six affirmations about what you have power of, when you are powerful, or why you have power.

Manifestation Statement: Make one, powerful statement about what you hope to manifest for your self-worth. Write it three times, each time making the words bigger on the page.

day 85

"Keep watering yourself, you're growing."
-E. Russell

Mindfulness: *Energy Ball.* Sit in a comfortable position with your legs and arms uncrossed, eyes closed. Starting with your toes, imagine a warm ball of energy moving up your body. Once the energy ball reaches the top of your head, return it to your third eye center (the space between your eyebrows). Imagine the ball of energy and visualize what color it is. Jot down what the experience was like in the space below.

Gratitude: *This Past Year.* List six things you are grateful for from this past year.

Affirmations: *Appearance.* Make six affirmations about your appearance.

Power Mantras for Abilities: Write two power mantras about your abilities.

day 86

"Letting go is an active process."
-Alicia Menendez

today's date: _____

starting mood: _____
ending mood: _____

Mindfulness: *Connect the Dots.* Starting from the left of the box below, connect the dots from left to right without lifting your pen from the page. You can draw up, down, diagonally, backward, and forward. Try to focus on each dot as you connect them. If your thoughts wander or if you notice yourself starting to make judgments, simply notice those thoughts and return to connecting the dots.

· ·
· ·
· ·
· ·

Gratitude: *Material items.* List six material items you are grateful for and why.

Affirmations: *Freebie.* Make your own category or prompts for what you will write affirmations about!

Month Ahead Manifestations: Think of something specific you hope to achieve. Maybe it's a dream you've had for a long time. Maybe it's a new goal you're working towards. Make statements like, "I will," or "I am going to," rather than "I hope to," or "I want to." Be specific with timing and words. Write it down in the space below. Say it out loud three times to really send it out into the universe.

day 87

"Everything has changed and yet, I am more me than I've ever been."
-Iain Thomas

starting mood: _____

today's date: _____   ending mood: _____

Mindfulness: *Free Doodle.* Set a timer for one minute. Doodle in the space provided. If your thoughts wander or if you notice yourself starting to make judgments about your doodling, simply notice those thoughts and return your attention to your drawing.

Gratitude: *Opportunities.* List four opportunities you have had or are going to have that you are grateful for.

Affirmations: *What You Attract.* Make six affirmations about positive experiences, material items, or relationships you attract.

Expectations   **Mini-Mantras**

day 88

"Fall in love with the process of becoming the very best version of yourself."

today's date: _____

starting mood: _____

ending mood: _____

Mindfulness: *Object Observation.* Set a timer for one minute. Choose an object in your line of sight. Using "beginner's mind," try to remain non-judgmental, meaning not adding any qualitative words to the observations you make. When the timer goes off, jot down what the experience was like for you.

Gratitude: *Life Right Now.* List six things you are grateful for in your life right now.

Affirmations: *Worth.* Make six affirmations about your worth.

Power Mantras for Wisdom: Write two power mantras about your inner wisdom.

day 89

"The soul usually knows what to do to heal itself. The challenge is to silence the mind."
-Caroline Myss

Mindfulness: *Energy Ball.* Sit in a comfortable position with your legs and arms uncrossed, eyes closed. Starting with your toes, imagine a warm ball of energy moving up your body. Once the energy ball reaches the top of your head, return it to your third eye center (the space between your eyebrows). Imagine the ball of energy and visualize what color it is. Jot down what the experience was like in the space below.

Gratitude: *This Past Month.* List six things you are grateful for from this past month.

Affirmations: *Accomplishments.* Write affirmations about your successes, your wins, and your accomplishments. You deserve it!

Manifestation Statement: Make one, powerful statement about what you hope to manifest for your self-worth. Write it three times, each time making the words bigger on the page.

day 90

"Self-love is becoming home to yourself, the same home you are to others."
-Dhiman

starting mood: _____

today's date: _____   ending mood: _____

Letter to Yourself: *Gratitude:* Write yourself a thank you letter for your time, energy, and commitment to this journaling practice.

congratulations, gorgeous.

you've completed your 90-day practice!

I can't imagine how wonderful you must feel for the work you've done in this journal. I hope you can look back and see the growth and change reflected in the pages. Take some time to solidify that growth and put your reflection into words.

In the space below, free-write about the last 90 days. How have you been impacted by this journal? How have you grown? What changes have occurred in your life because of this practice?

faq's

How long does each journal take?
Each entry takes about 5-10 minutes—that's it! Sometimes it takes less time, sometimes more—it all depends on the prompts, your mood, and how focused you feel.

Is it ok to do it at different times of the day?
I find that doing it at the same time of day creates a habit, which makes it more likely that I'll do it on a daily basis. Doing it in the morning sets me up for the rest of the day—by the time it's afternoon I've already missed out on several hours where the gratitude or re-framing expectations could have come in handy. This is why I recommend users practice in the morning, but again it's your practice, so do it when it feels best for you!

This sounds like a lot of work. is it hard?
It is hard starting out—as someone who struggles deeply with anxiety, depression, and low self-esteem, these are all activities that are gut-wrenchingly annoying and tedious. At first it felt almost pointless. I remember thinking "I'm not really grateful for this shit," or "I don't actually believe I'm pretty or cool." But the more I practiced the exercises in this journal, the easier it became, and the more I noticed myself feeling calm, confident, and optimistic on a daily basis.

Where are all these categories from?
The prompts and categories are a collection of tools I learned over the last decade in therapy and as a graduate counseling student. They come from Zen Mindfulness practices, Dialectical Behavior Therapy, Cognitive Behavioral Therapy, Rational Emotion Behavior Therapy, spiritual practices, and Existential Therapy.

What if I can't think of something for the prompt?
That's ok! I invite you to be super kind to yourself if (and when) this happens. I still struggle sometimes to answer certain prompts, even if they are prompts I see all the time. Our brains get tired, we have off days, and life is simply not linear.

feeling stuck?

Here are some suggestions!

Ask yourself what a loved one might say.

Skip this prompt and return to it at the end of the practice.

Ask yourself what Oprah would say (I'm serious).

Think about what Rachel might respond with.

Leave it blank. This is for YOU—not for me, not for your mom or dad, not for anyone else. If something isn't resonating, say, "welp, that shit's not for me today!" and move on!

thank you!

Darling self-healer, thank you so much for investing in this journal, and investing in yourself. I hope you found this experience insightful, meaningful, and encouraging. You deserve a beautiful, whole, and rich life. I invite you to continue investing in yourself and giving yourself the gift of healing. You deserve it.

copyright notice

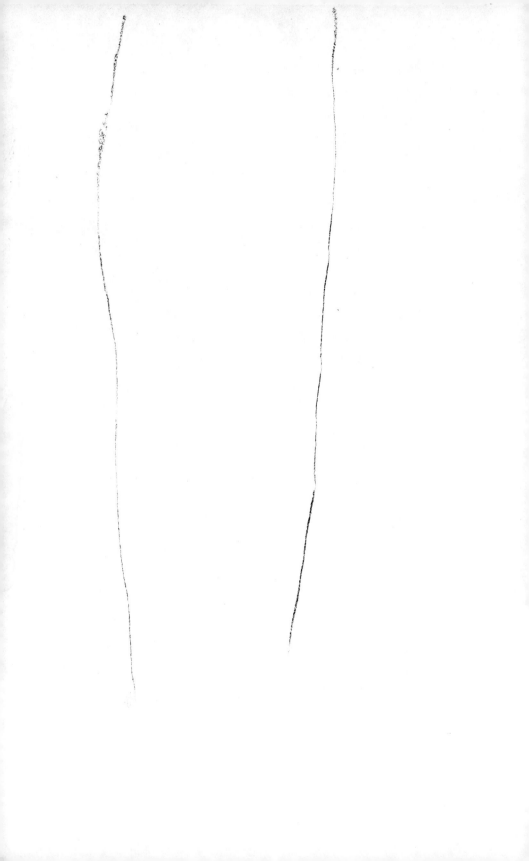

CPSIA information can be obtained
at www.ICGtesting.com
Printed in the USA
BVHW021517281021
620179BV00020B/500

9 781087 906676